SILENT KILLERS

The Robber
John 10:10

By
Pamela Hackett

PAMELA HACKETT

Copyright © 2019 by Pamela Hackett

SILENT KILLERS

Dedication

SILENT KILLERS

I dedicate this book to Julia Neal Daily and Global Outreach Ministries and Training Center.

Table of Contents

SILENT KILLERS

Introduction
Chapter One - People
Chapter Two - Dust
Chapter Three - Sifting
Chapter Four - Worrying
Chapter Five - Overwhelm
Chapter Six - Recede
Chapter Seven - Ignorance
Chapter Eight - Pride
Chapter Nine - Hope Deferred
Chapter Ten - Deception
Chapter Eleven - Self-Deception
Chapter Twelve - Distraction
Chapter Thirteen - Heartache
Chapter Fourteen - Love
Chapter Fifteen - Isolation
Chapter Sixteen - Sweep Under the Rug
Chapter Seventeen - Fear
Prayer
Notes

Introduction

SILENT KILLERS

A *Silent Killer* is a *noun*.

A person, a place, or thing.

This book, "*Silent Killers*", came about through intercession. While praying for someone in my devotional time with the Lord I began to hear the Holy Spirit say, "log onto Facebook and create a live video". Upon doing so I asked viewers if they currently have a *Silent Killer* or *Killers* in their lives. I prayed and as the scripture states in Mark 5:9, the *Silent Killer was* robbing them of their life and they could not see it. I immediately heard the Holy Spirit say, "write".

Warn my people for many do not know that they have a spirit in their lives that is "silent" and a robber.

John 10:10 says, "for the thief comes to steal, kill and destroy".

Each of the *Silent Killers* will lead to another *Silent Killer* if it's not detected by a physical doctor or simply by spending time in the presence of the Holy Spirit. It will go unnoticed.

Silent Killers

When I googled *Silent Killers* this is what I found.

Definition

Hypertension or high blood pressure is also famously called a *Silent Killer* and for good reason. It makes no health sense to ignore a *Silent Killer*.

Breast cancer is a *Silent Killer* and raising awareness is the key to winning the battle against this disease.

This stems from a medical standpoint of *Silent Killers*.

The dictionary definition of *Silent Killers* states:

A disease that has no obvious symptoms or indications.

Symptoms

1. Silent
2. Hushed
3. Muted
4. Noiseless
5. Quiet
6. Soundless
7. Still
8. Stilly (poetic).

It can cause one to be dumb, mum, mute, non-vocal, not talkative, speechless, stuck dumb, taciturn, tongue tied, uncommunicative, unspeaking, voiceless, and wordless.

The Spiritual definition of a *Silent Killer* states

SILENT KILLERS

this: The Holy Spirit said this Silent Killer can be compared to carbon monoxide.

Let's take a look.

Carbon Monoxide

A colorless, odorless, very toxic gas (CO) that is formed as a product of the incomplete combustion of carbon or a carbon compound.

It's a *noun*.

Symptoms

1. Dull headache
2. Weakness
3. Dizziness
4. Nausea or vomiting
5. Shortness of breath
6. Confusion
7. Blurred vision
8. Loss of consciousness

The person I was praying for exemplified each one of the symptoms identified by Holy Spirit.

PAMELA HACKETT

Chapter One
People

SILENT KILLERS

Human beings individually or collectively.

Symptoms

1. People
2. Spouse
3. Children
4. Boss
5. Co-worker

Scripture

Psalm 18:29

For by thee I have run through a troop; and by my God have I leaped over a wall.

You may ask yourself, "how are people considered *Silent Killers?*"

The Bible says, "know them who labor among you". Many times we do not pay attention to the role of those in our lives but I've come to alert you. When people come into our lives and leave us feeling depleted, stressed or worried they are identified as a *Silent Killer*. Before interacting with them our peace and joy are intact but the moment they leave we feel stressed. Like John 10:10, they are robbing us of our life but I say to you, rise up in the strength of the Great Detector, the Holy Spirit and begin to run through those troops.

PAMELA HACKETT

If you don't, you will find yourself in a hospital room, with all forms of health problems. Put them in their place of being silent, because if you don't, they will put you in a place!!!

Beware.

SILENT KILLERS

Chapter Two
Dust

SILENT KILLERS

Fine, dry powder consisting of tiny particles of earth or waste matter lying on the ground or on surfaces or carried in the air.

Symptoms

1. Dirt
2. Grime
3. Filth
4. Smut
5. Soot
6. Fine powder

An act of dusting.

Scripture

Matthew 10:14

If anyone will not welcome you to listen to your words, leave that home or town and shake the dust off your feet.

The dust this scripture speaks of, are the little things in life that we allow to settle and leave unchecked. We've allowed thought patterns and life's circumstances to linger.

Naturally, dust can build up in our home when we don't pay attention. Weeks and months pass by and dust builds up. In the beginning we can't see it. We breathe it in until we sneeze and say to ourselves, "why is it, every time I come into this room my allergies begin to act up?" Easy answer, we can't always detect dust.

Spiritually, when people give us advice, we may start coughing, having breathing problems, headache and our allergies are all out of whack. Each time someone addresses the dust in our lives these symptoms start all over again. They are stirring up the dust in our lives.

Let me say this, the only way we can detect this *Silent Killer* is by the Holy Spirit. Don't be like those that choose to die in the curse. Receive the remedy of the advice and allow the Holy Spirit to clean you up.

Also, we must recognize when we can are giving advice/ministering to people who ultimately have no desire to receive what we are saying.

It's time to do the dust dance.

Ready! Set! GO!

Chapter Three
Sifting

SILENT KILLERS

An act of sifting something, especially so as to isolate that which is most important or useful.

Symptoms

1. To separate or remove
2. To scatter
3. To break up
4. To examine closely
5. To question closely

Scripture

Luke 22:31-34

And the Lord said, Simon! Simon! Indeed Satan has asked for you, that he may sift you as wheat.

But I have prayed for you; that your faith should not fail; and when you have returned to me, strengthen your brethren.

But he said to him, Lord I am ready to go with you, both to prison and to death.

Then he said, I tell you. Peter, the rooster shall not crow this day before you will deny three times that you know me.

Most people never recognize the moments they are being sifted; it is silent. A strong prayer life and a relationship with the Great Detector, Holy Spirit, and taking the time to listen and hear what the Holy Spirit is saying about the situation is necessary. Sifting moves us away from what God has called us to do. It doesn't start the day we recognize it; it starts the first day the situation occurs.

Instead of being sifted like wheat, let us put sifting in a grinder, grind it up and call forth the wind to blow it away forever!!!

Beware.

Chapter Four
Worrying

SILENT KILLERS

Causing anxiety about actual or potential problems alarming.

Worry

To give way to anxiety or unease; allow one's mind to dwell on difficulty or trouble.

Symptoms

1. Fret
2. Be concerned
3. Be anxious
4. Antagonize
5. Overthink
6. Brood
7. Panic
8. Lose sleep
9. Get worked up
10. Get stressed
11. Stew
12. Torment oneself
13. Trouble
14. Bother
15. Make anxious
16. Disturb
17. Distresses
18. Upset concern
19. Play on one's mind
20. Weigh down

Scripture

Philippians 4:6-8

Be anxious for nothing, but in everything by prayer and supplication, with thanksgiving, let your requests be made known to God.

And the peace of which surpasses all understanding will guard your hearts and minds through Christ Jesus.

John 14:1

Let not your hearts be troubled, believe in God, believe also in me.

The Word tell us not to worry but we always find ourselves in a place of worrying about this or that. When we allow worry to consume us, after a period of time, worry takes full control. We finally say to ourselves, "I'll just give it to the Lord". In reality, we have allowed worry to work perfectly in us. We must remember to align with the Word. Philippians 4:6-7 says, "Don't worry about anything instead we should pray, tell God what we are in need of and when we begin to do that worry cannot stand. We will begin to experience the peace of God that surpasses all understanding". When a situation arises in our lives, let's lift it up before God before we speak out loud. Once we speak out loud, the enemy uses it as a weapon without our knowledge.

SILENT KILLERS

Let us align with the Word and close the door on this *Silent Killer*!!!!!

Beware.

Chapter Five
Overwhelm

To bury or drown beneath a huge mass.

Symptoms

1. Swamp
2. Submerge
3. Engulf
4. Bury
5. Deluge
6. Flood
7. Inundate.

Defeat (utterly/heavily), rout beat (hollow), conquer, vanquish, be victorious over, triumph over worst, overcome, overthrow and crush.

Scripture

Psalm 61:2

From the ends of the earth I call to you, I call as my heart grows faint, lead me to the rock that is higher than I.

Psalm 28:7

The Lord is my strength and my shield; my heart trusts in him and I am helped. My heart leaps for joy and I will give thanks to him in song.

While writing this book, I came under attack by the *Silent Killer overwhelm*. It was one of the worst feelings I have ever felt in my stomach and I stopped writing for days at a time. To be overwhelmed by something usually causes you to be still. This is what happened to me, I couldn't move forward in my God-given assignment.

As a result, a new *Silent Killer* manifested called *recede*. I heard the Holy Spirit whisper the word, *"recede"* one morning. I began to ask the Lord what it meant and this is what he showed me.

Chapter Six
Recede

SILENT KILLERS

Go or move back or further away from a previous position.

Symptoms

1. Retreat
2. Go back
3. Go down
4. Move back
5. Move away
6. Withdraw
7. Ebb
8. Subside

Scripture

Luke 9:62

And Jesus said unto him, no man, having put his hand to the plough, and looking back, is fit for the kingdom of God.

This is what I experienced. I began to diminish. Slowly, day after day and slowly but surely I moved away from writing this book. For days, I looked at the book and walked past it.

The Holy Spirit gave me many prophetic visions of *recede* and how I had allowed the *Silent Killer recede* to take root.

He (Holy Spirit) gave me the word "sleep" and He said, "the type of sleep you are experiencing is not normal. When a person sleeps they are non-active. The sleep that you are experiencing allows people to walk around wide awake but are asleep to the assignment that I have called them to".

This *Silent Killer* caused me to subside and move away. Through prayer I began to rise again to finish the assignment given to me.
Beware.

Chapter Seven
Ignorance

SILENT KILLERS

Lack of knowledge or information.

Symptoms

1. Incomprehension of unawareness or unconsciousness of unfamiliarity with
2. Inexperience with
3. Lack of knowledge about
4. Lack of information about

Scripture

Hosea 4:6

My people are destroyed for lack of knowledge: because thou hast rejected knowledge, I will also reject them that thou shalt be no priest to me. Seeing thou hast forgotten the law of thy God, I will also forget thy children.

Get knowledge, get understanding.

My people are destroyed for lack of knowledge.

Where there is no knowledge, we walk in darkness. When we begin to gain knowledge, it sheds light into the darkness, and darkness dissipates. Gaining knowledge, understanding and walking in knowledge changes the ball game. Let's cause ignorance to take a permanent place of silence so that we can rise up out of a dark place of destruction, to a place called Victory!!!
Beware.

PAMELA HACKETT

Chapter Eight
Pride

SILENT KILLERS

A feeling or deep pleasure or satisfaction derived from one's own achievements, the achievement of those with whom one is closely associated or from qualities and possessions that are widely admired.

Symptoms

1. Pleasure
2. Joy
3. Delight
4. Gratification
5. Fulfillment
6. Satisfaction

Scripture

Proverbs 16:18

Pride goes before destruction, a haughty spirit before a fall.

James 4:10

Humble yourselves before the Lord and he will lift you up.

If we are not aware of the *Silent Killer* called pride we will be susceptible to falling. When pride operates in a person's life it leads to a place of destruction. People usually refuse to see it.

Pride will cause a person to be blinded where they can't see themselves. They go into a fallen place but once they recognize it, they can put pride in its proper place and cause it to be destroyed.

When pride is not dealt with it will take us to a fallen place. It's time to recognize the *Silent Killer* and rise up in true humility. It will cause the spirit of pride to be defeated.

Remember the robber is a thief and he wants to steal from us.

Beware.

Chapter Nine
Hope Deferred

SILENT KILLERS

Makes the heart sick.

Symptoms

1. Despair
2. Setback
3. Defeat
4. Failure
5. Frustration
6. Let down
7. Come down

Scripture

Proverbs 13:12

Hope deferred makes the heart sick but a longing fulfilled is a tree of life.

Hope deferred comes to destroy our plans either naturally and spiritually. Whenever something enters our lives through a loss of finances, a loss of a job, death, etc., it sends us into a place called deferred. The situation begins to render us hopeless and causes the heart to become sick. It is time for us to recognize the silent things in our lives leading us to a deferred place called hopelessness.

Let's make hope deferred null and void in our lives!!!

Beware.

Chapter Ten
Deception

SILENT KILLERS

The action of deceiving someone

Symptoms

1. Deceit
2. Deceitfulness
3. Duplicity
4. Double-dealing fraud
5. Cheating
6. Trickery
7. Chicanery
8. Slyness
9. Gulie
10. Bluff
11. Lying

Scripture

Galatians 6:7-8

Be not deceived; God is not mocked: For whatsoever a man soweth, that he shall also reap.

James 1:22

But be ye doers of the words and not hearers only, deceiving your own selves.

Deception, the great Silent Killer, is just one of them. It will lead us down the wrong road. Everything we do can be done because of deception. It will encompass us no matter what people tell us. We refuse to believe deception is a robber and some never get on the right track until something seriously happens in their lives.

It's time to spend time with the Great Detector, the Holy Spirit. He will lead and guide us into truth.

Beware.

Chapter Eleven
Self-Deception

SILENT KILLERS

The action or practice of allowing oneself to believe that a false or invalidated feeling, idea, or situation is true.

Self-deception is the act of lying to yourself or making yourself believe something that isn't really true.

Symptoms

1. Deception
2. Fantasy
3. Daydream
4. Trickery
5. False impression
6. Shade
7. Illusion
8. Error
9. Misapprehension
10. Oversight.

Scripture

1 Corinthians 3:18-20

Let no man deceive himself. If any man among you seem to be wise in this world let him become a fool, that he may be wise.

Proverbs 12:15

The ways of a fool is right in his own eyes but a wise man is he who listens to counsel

Self-deception is an ancient spirit and it has been around a long time. It weakens our resolve concerning truth that we know and can cause us to begin to lean unto our own understanding. The Great Detector, the Holy Spirit, will keep us from falling to self-deception; as long as we are willing to connect with Him daily. As we walk in obedience we will begin to notice a difference.

Let's put this robber in jail for LIFE!

Beware.

Chapter Twelve
Distraction

SILENT KILLERS

A thing that prevents someone from giving full attention to someone else.

Symptoms

1. Diversion
2. Interruption
3. Disturbance
4. Interference
5. Hindrance

Extreme agitation of the mind or emotions.

Frenzy, hysteria, mental distress, madness, insanity.

Scripture

Proverbs 4:25

Look straight ahead and fix your eyes on what lies before you.

1 Peter 5:8

Be sober, be vigilant; because your adversary, the devil, as a roaring lion, walks about seeking whom he may devour.

Hebrews 12:2

Fixing our attention on Jesus, the pioneer and perfecter of our faith.

2 Corinthians 6:14

Do not be yoked together with unbelievers. For what do righteousness and wickedness have in common? Or what fellowship can light have with darkness?

Distraction comes to move us off of our God intended path. Something always finds its way to interfere with our progress. We must take the time to fix our eyes on what lies before us while refusing to move to the left or right and keep our focus. No matter what happens around us.

It's time for us to send distraction on the run.

Beware.

Chapter Thirteen
Heartache

SILENT KILLERS

Emotional anguish or grief, typically caused by the loss or absence of someone loved.

Symptoms

1. Anguish
2. Grief
3. Suffering
4. Distress
5. Unhappiness
6. Misery
7. Sorrow
8. Sadness
9. Hurt
10. Pain

Scripture

Proverbs 15:13

A joyful heart makes a cheerful face, but when the heart is sad the spirit is broken.

Proverbs 13:12

Hope deferred makes the heart sick, but desires fulfilled is a tree of life.

Proverbs 34:18

The Lord is near to the brokenhearted and saves those who are crushed in spirit.

Where there's an aching in the heart, it can lead to death. If there's a broken heart there's no life. Sadness and pain always comes to rob us. It's time to bury the aching of the heart and put it in a coffin so that joy may arise and cause us to live.

It's time to bury the aching heart. Let's begin to mount up.

Arise.

Chapter Fourteen
Love

SILENT KILLERS

An intense feeling of deep affection.

Symptoms

1. Fondness
2. Tenderness
3. Warmth
4. Intimacy
5. Attachment

Scripture

1 Corinthians 13:4-8

Love is patient, love is kind. It does not envy, it does not boast it is not proud.

It does not dishonor others, it is not self-seeking it is not easily angered, it keeps no record of wrongs.

Love does not delight in evil but rejoices with the truth.

It always protects, always trusts, always hopes, and always preserves.

Love never fails.

1 John 4:18

There is no fear in love, but perfect love drives out fear because fear has to do with punishment. The one who fears is not made perfect in love.

Signs of unhealthy love:

1. Lack of communication
2. Loss of emotional intimacy
3. Disengagement
4. Inability to forgive
5. Codependent behavior
6. Substance abuse
7. Verbal abuse
8. Physical abuse
9. Loss of respect for self
10. Not standing for yourself

An unhealthy love is very dangerous.

It can lead to depression and suicide which are *Silent Killers*. Beware when love begins to turn sour.

Take action quickly!

Don't allow this *Silent Killer* to kill you.

Seek help immediately and get out!

Chapter Fifteen
Isolation

SILENT KILLERS

The state of one who is alone, may imply a condition of being apart from all human being or being off by wish or circumstance from one's unusual associate. Detachment from others involuntarily, shutting away or keeping apart from others often connoting, deliberate withdrawal from the world.

Symptoms

1. Separation
2. Withdrawal
3. Loneliness
4. Detachment
5. Solitude

Scripture

Psalms 34:17-19

Is anyone crying for help? God is listening. Ready to rescue you if your heart is broken, you'll find God right there, if you've been kicked in the gut, he'll help you catch your breath.

Disciples so often still get into trouble, God is always there.

Proverb 18:1

And I'm friendly person isolates himself and seems to care only about his own issues, for his contempt of sound judgment makes him a recluse.

Proverbs 11:14

Without good direction, people lose their way, the more wise counsel, the better and your chances.

Isolation loves wounded and hurt people. When we withdraw from people and places or detach ourselves from the community. The wounds are magnified and seem to hurt more because we aren't willing to speak about them. This *Silent Killer* causes us to go into a place of separating ourselves from people to the point, the enemy makes us feel lonely and it gives him the opportunity to move in. Next, the pain goes even deeper and we never desire to return to that place of healing. We must be willing to talk about it. Depression and suicide sneaks in along with many other dysfunctional thoughts. I advise everyone to seek help personally, mentally and spiritually.

It is time to rise with the help of a counselors or therapist and come out of the fallen place called isolation and let it steal no more.

Beware.

Chapter Sixteen

Fear

SILENT KILLERS

"Fear will cause you to make wrong decisions".

-Dr. Venner Alston

Unpleasant emotion caused by the belief that someone or something is dangerous and likes to cause pain or threat.

To be afraid of someone or something that likely can be dangerous.

Symptoms

1. Terror
2. Fright
3. Fearfulness
4. Horror
5. Alarm
6. Panic
7. Agitation
8. Trepidation
9. Dread
10. Consternation
11. Dismay
12. Distress
13. Be afraid of
14. Be fearful of
15. Be scared of
16. Be apprehensive
17. Live in fear of

Scripture

2 Timothy 1:7

For God has not given us a spirit of fear but of power, and of love and of a sound mind.

Fear is the deceiver of us all. It hides within our personality and keeps us from speaking when needed. We tend to hold things in that ultimately begin to eat away at our soul, mind, will, and emotions. I can recall days where fear had me in places of being double minded (no sound mind) and making wrong decisions; I should have said no but instead, I said yes over and over again. Fear causes us to miss the blessing that God has for us.

Let's put this *Silent Killer* in a blender and blend up fear so that we can rise up in true power, love and a sound mind.

Let's put fear under our feet and squash it, smash it, and say GOODBYE!

Chapter Seventeen

Swept Under the Rug

SILENT KILLERS

To ignore, deny, or conceal from public's view or knowledge. Something that is embarrassing, unappealing or damaging to one's reputation.

Symptoms

1. Conceal
2. Hide
3. Suppress
4. Ignite
5. Keep silent about
6. Keep dark
7. Hush up

Scripture

James 5:16

Confess our faults one to another, and pray one for another that you may be healed. The effectual fervent prayer of a righteous man avails much.

This *Silent Killer* is silent when we walk in unbelief and refuse to deal with the matter at hand. We try to silence this by sending it in another direction. Or we simply use the old, familiar pattern and sweep this under the rug. A rug has the tendency to move when walked over it.

It's time to take the spiritual vacuum out on this issue so that we can stop hiding things under the rug.

Beware.

SILENT KILLERS

Hear me! Every one of these *Silent Killers* are thieves and robbers. They come to rob you of your destiny. They can also cause you to have a physical illness.

Be watchful.

Be on the lookout.

Be alert.

If the doctor can or cannot explain the symptoms; look in this book, the Bible and consult Holy Spirit.

You just may have a *Silent Killer* in your life.

Blessings!

PAMELA HACKETT

SILENT KILLERS

Prayer

Father give us eyes to see the *Silent Killers* in our lives that have come to rob us of our peace and joy. Let us see the thief that comes to steal, kill and destroy us of our destiny in Jesus name.

Amen.

Pamela Hackett
Your Awareness Coach

SILENT KILLERS
NOTES

www.ingramcontent.com/pod-product-compliance
Lightning Source LLC
Chambersburg PA
CBHW071414290426
44108CB00014B/1821